calligraphy
AND
hand lettering
FOR BEGINNERS

Illustrated by Karina Krivenko

WELCOME,
ASPIRING CALLIGRAPHER!

The impact of a message depends upon the way that message is presented. Michelangelo's Sistine Chapel ceiling fills us with awe; the words "In the beginning God created the heaven and the earth," written on this page present the same message, but with infinitely less emotional impact.

In the early fifth century, Christian monks found a middle way for those who could not quite equal the artistic genius of Michelangelo to nonetheless add emotional impact to the messages they wished to communicate. These ordinary monks devoted their lives to applying readily learned handwriting and calligraphy skills to produce beautifully illuminated manuscripts, multiplying the emotional power of the Bible and other religious texts.

A thousand years later, the printing press made it possible to exchange the beauty of these rare illuminated manuscripts with millions of mass-produced texts. In our own day, the internet revolution has similarly made it possible to replace beautifully hand-written personal notes with standard-font messages sent simultaneously to dozens or hundreds of individuals.

The teaching of cursive writing may be slowly disappearing from grade-school curricula, but a growing number of individuals, refusing to sacrifice the beauty and grace of handwriting, are turning their attention to the calligraphic arts.

The inexpressible benefit of being able to express one's thoughts in a beautiful hand comes at a remarkably small cost: inexpensive and readily available pens, ink, and paper. And however much time one wishes to devote, from a decade of study under an old master to some weeks or months learning from a text, or somewhere in between. Practice a bit each day, and before long the beautiful curve in your mind's eye will present itself routinely on the page in front of you.

You will find a surprising variety of ways to express your newly-learned handwriting skills: personal letters, wedding invitations, graduation announcements, business cards, bookmarks. Do not be surprised if friends and family call upon you for beautiful handwriting; you might even find yourself with a side-business if you so choose.

THE TOOLS

Stop by your local art store (or go online) and put together a basic writing tool kit. It won't cost much. After you're comfortable writing with this basic kit you'll likely want to explore new nibs, new inks, and writing with brushes.

We recommend you start with these:

1) a 3.8 mm Pilot Parallel (Fountain) Pen

This pen is comfortable in the hand (allowing you to concentrate on your form), produces a crisp and clear line and remarkable color-effects, takes up just the right amount of space on the page, and comes apart easily for cleaning. You don't have to carry around different nibs, holders, and inks: just pick it up and write.

Use fountain pen-ink with this pen. Or try acrylic ink, but then be sure to clean your pen often. India ink is too clogging and it can ruin the pen.

Every broad-edged hand in this book was written with the 3.8 mm Pilot.

After your hand feels comfortable with the 3.8 mm Pilot Parallel pen you might want to try the 1.5 mm, 2.4 mm, or 6.0 mm Pilot for a different look.

An advanced beginner might like to razor-slice the tip of the 6.0 mm pen for a double-stroke or triple-stroke effect.

The next items for your toolkit are a nib, a holder, and ink.

2) *Metal Nibs*

Broad-edged (chiseled) nibs set down the broader lines typical of classic calligraphy styles such as Gothic, Humanistic cursive, Uncial, and many others.

You may want to try a broad-edged nib with a straight tip or a slanted tip, or even a "left-handed" nib that makes it look like your writing is "slanting backwards."

Brause broad-edged calligraphy nibs are perfect for both the beginner and the experienced hand.

Pointed nibs create the thin, spare "English Copperplate" and "American Spencerian" scripts and are essential for certain contemporary calligraphic styles.

The Nikko G is a resilient, durable nib which will easily accommodate your efforts to apply ink to paper with just the right amount of pressure.

After your hand is comfortable with the Nikko G, a world of nibs awaits you!

3) *Holder*

Holders come in every style for every taste. Pick out what you like. And pick up a separate holder for each nib.

4) *Ink*

Non-waterproof ink can set down a thinner line and is easier to remove from the nib. Black ink for best contrast and visibility. Colored ink for variety and fun.

5) *Paper*

Practice on smooth, plain, white (but not shiny) paper, such as layout paper. Your serious work belongs on thick paper that wouldn't dream of wrinkling on you. Use hot-pressed paper if you're making a comissioned project. Use highly textured or homemade paper for large textural letters. Make sure the ink you're using won't bleed onto the paper you want to buy.

Arch
the curved stroke springing from the stem.

Ascender
the part of a minuscule that extends above the x-height.

Baseline
the horizontal line on which a letter sits.

Bowl
a part of a letter with an enclosed curve.

Capital line
the writing line to which uppercase letters rise.

Crossbar
the horizontal stroke on a letter.

Cursive
a faster script with fewer pen lifts and inclining toward handwriting.

Descender
the part of a minuscule that extends below the x-height.

Diamond
a single stroke mark made by a broad-edged pen when held at 30° or 45° pen angle.

Downstroke
a stroke commencing at the top of the x-height or ascender height and finishing at the bottom of the x-height or the descender height.

Ductus
the order, number, and directions of strokes to create a finished letter.

Ear
a small stroke to the right of g.

Flourish
a decorative extension to a letter — usually an ascender or descender, but also a majuscule or termination).

Hairline
the thinnest mark that a pen can make.

Majuscule
(capital, upper case)
a large letter originally derived from the letters of Ancient Rome.

Minuscule
(lower case)
a small character.

Monoline
a line of consistent width, with the same stem thickness vertically and horizontally.

Ligature
the linking of letters by one or more strokes.

Loop
the enclosed space in an ascender or descender.

Pen width
the width of the mark made by pen when held at 90 to the writing line. It is used to determine measurements for the x-height, ascenders, and descenders.

Reservoir
a small metal fitting that allows a nib to hold extra ink.

Stem
the main part of a letter, usually the vertical or diagonal stroke.

Stroke
a straight or a curved line made by the pen.

Tail
the diagonal stroke of R and Q.

Upstroke
a fine thin line. It usually refers to pointed pen hairlines.

x-height
the height of the body of the letter without ascender or descender.

If calligraphy was a religion (and who said it isn't) its most honored saint would be an Englishman from the early 1900's: Edward Johnston. This artist devoted his afternoons to the British Museum studying manuscripts, and it is there that he might have come across a book of Psalms written in a hand from the days of Charlemagne, which he modified slightly to create the beautifully rounded "Foundational" hand. A perfect hand, as we have noted, for the beginning calligrapher.

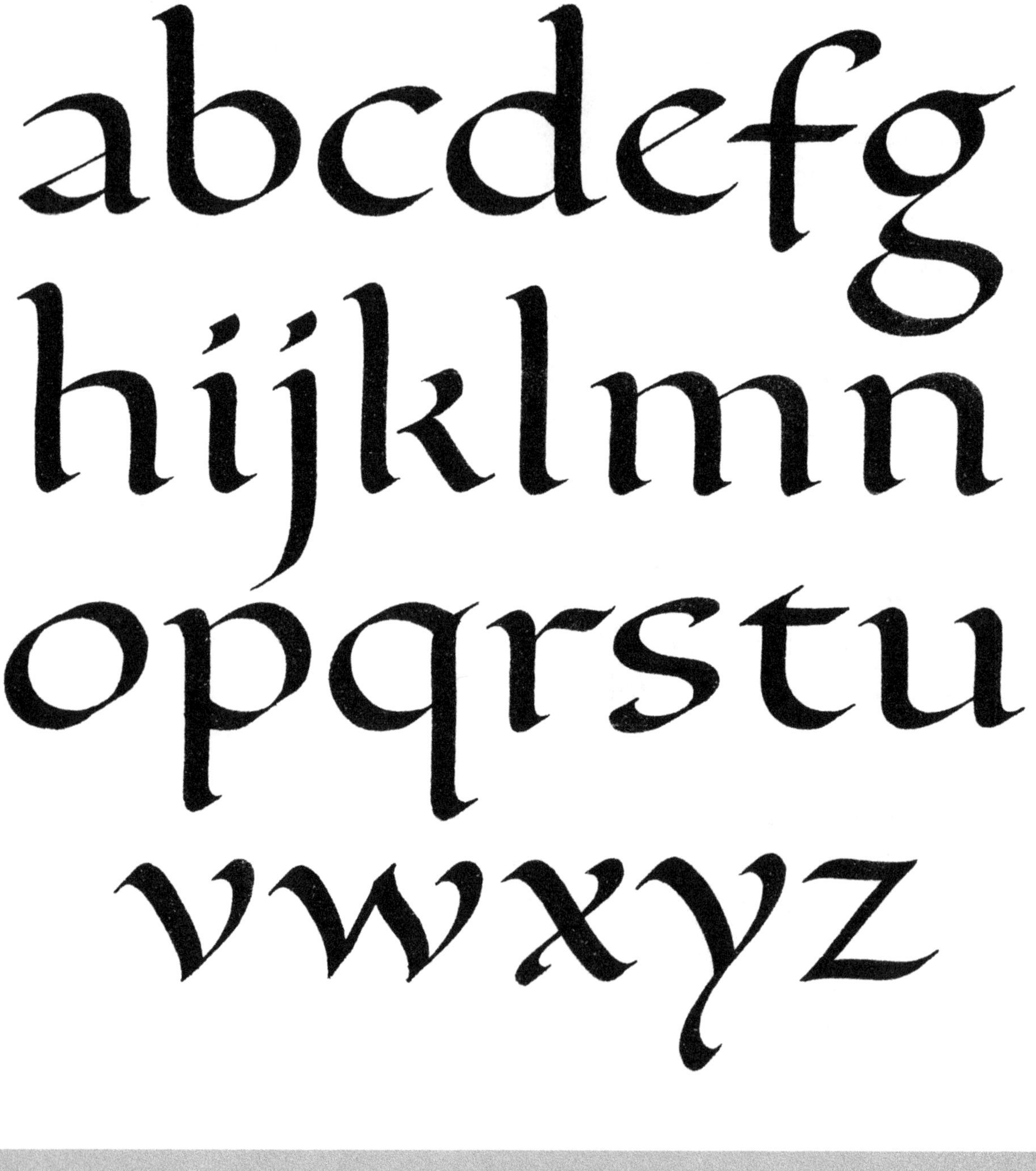

Key Points

pen angle: mainly 30°
x-height: four + three (for ascenders and descenders) pen widths
rhythm: undulating and round with equidistant parallels
O: based on a circle

Limber up your hands and fingers. Gently close and open your hands, twirl your fingers, twiddle your thumbs, to make your hands and fingers happy and ready to carry your beautifully-conceived letters to the page. You'll be writing from left to right and from the top down, applying equal pressure to the left and the right sides of the nib.

You can practice writing the Foundational Hand (or any broad-edged alphabet) by wrapping two pencils together with masking tape, especially when you're practicing writing big letters. Brighten your letters by coloring them in.

You will make the quickest progress by writing the letters in family groups:
I group — i, l, j, t, u, r, n, m, f, h, b, p, k
O group — o, c, e, d, q, a, g, s
V group — v, w, x, y, z

i

l

j

t

u

r

n

m

f

h

k

a

c

e

o

d

q

b

p

g

s

v

w

x

y

z

foundational

And now you will want to add to your basic tool kit. Practice the Foundational Hand, and the next hands we will discuss (Roman, Gothic) with the Pilot Parallel 2.4mm Pen or with one of these metal nibs: Brause 2.5mm, Tape 2.5mm, or Speedball C2.

The Roman or Latin Hand, used by over a billion people, is the world's most common hand. You're reading it now, and it's an important hand for you to master. The most influential example of the Roman Hand is found at the base of an early second century column monument to the Roman Emperor Trajan's victory over an enemy from the other side of the Danube.

ABCDEF
GHIJKL
MNOPQ
RSTU
VWXYZ

Key Points

pen angles: uprights 30°, diagonals 45°, horizontals 20°
x-height: eight pen widths
rhythm: space between letters is based on the volume of internal space
O: based on a circle

H

N

A

V

E

F

L

C

G

O

Q

D

M

W

T

U

Z

K

P

R

B

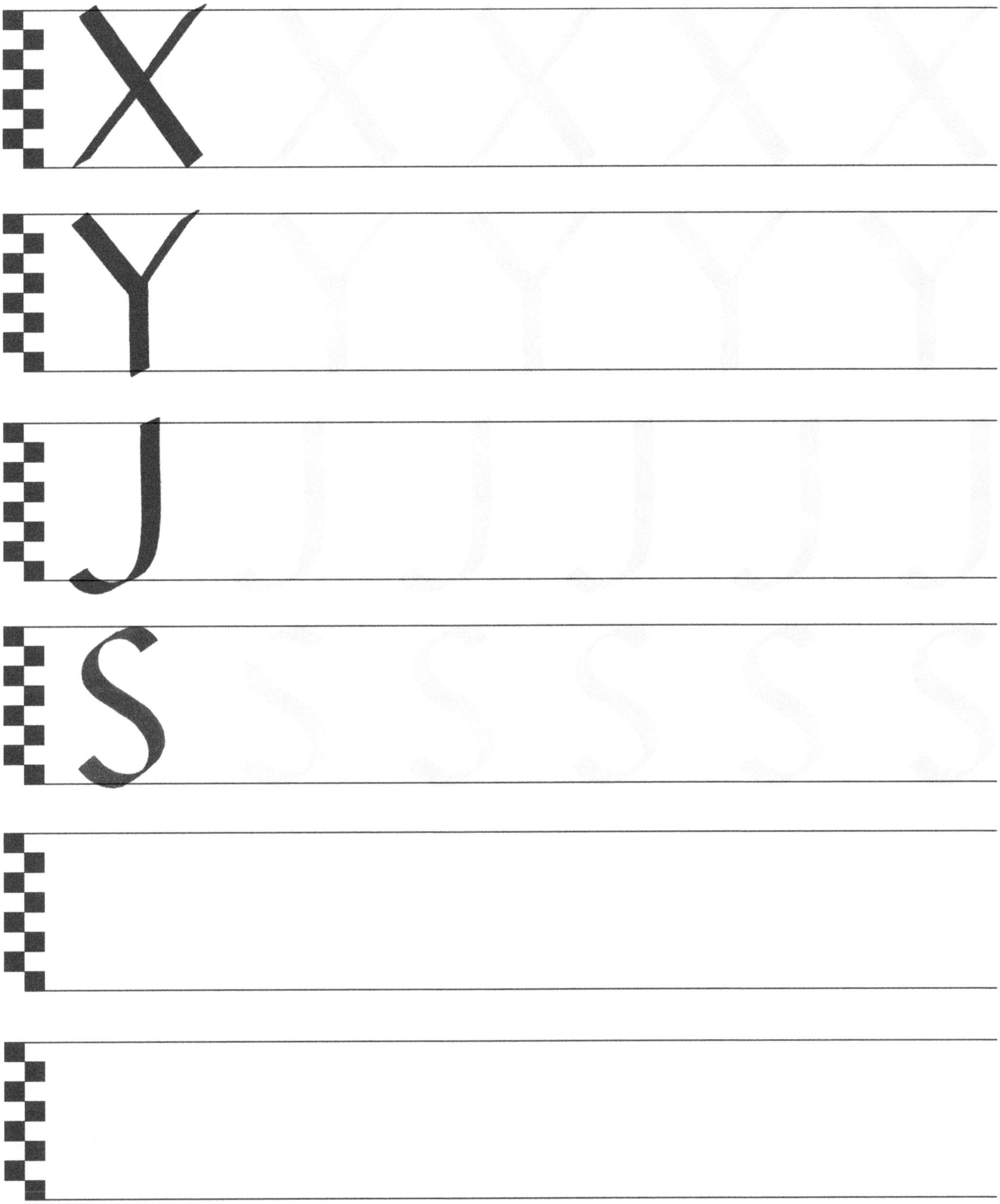

Close relatives of the majuscule (capital) letters found on Trajan's column are paired with many different types of minuscule (small) hands, including our friend the Foundational. You will find Roman variations with such intriguing names as flourished, manipulated, squat, chunky, spare, and even polyrhythmic.

The letters were chiseled out of stone and then painted over. So they had to be modified a bit for the calligrapher's pen and paper.

Note that the heights of the Capitals are lower than the heights of the ascenders.

These guidelines are designed to practice Roman Capitals alongside Foundational minuscules. Reccomended pen: Pilot Parallel 2.4mm. If you feel like writing with a traditional metal nib, switch to a Brause 2.5mm, Tape 2.5mm, or Speedball C2.

Calligraphy is sometimes a struggle between ease of reading and beauty. In the Gothic Hand, ease of reading has clearly lost the struggle to the goal of creating a beautiful texture in letters. If you increase the distance between letters more than a slight amount (to increase readability), the essential feeling of Gothic texture disappears. Gothic letters belong together, so write them in groups.

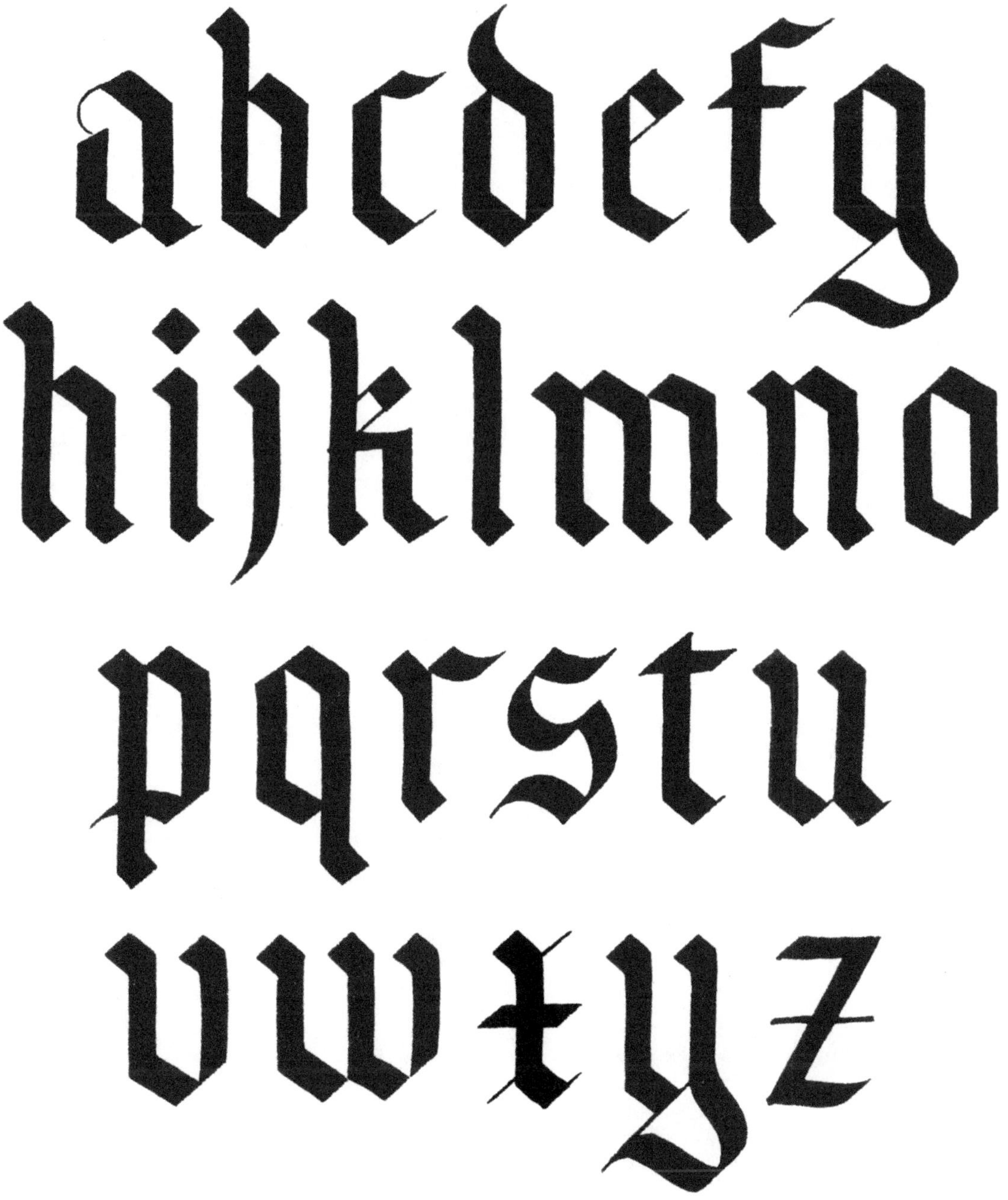

Key Points

pen angle: 45°
x-height: four + two (for ascenders and descenders) pen widths
rhythm: equidistant parallels
O: based on a compressed hexagon

Have a look at the many Gothic hands, some of which date to the 12th century: Textus Prescissus, Textura Quadrata, Rotunda, and Fraktur. The Gothic Hand was standard in Denmark until 1875, and in Germany until the 1930s.

blackletter

n

m

b

p

h

c

e

o

a

q

d

g

u

y

v

w

f

blackletter

a a a a a a a a a

z z z z z z z z z

s s s s s s s s s

s s s s s s s s s

Gothic minuscules can be frighteningly dense. To prevent the capitals from disappearing entirely, calligraphers tend to decorate them with diamonds, ticks, or added lines.

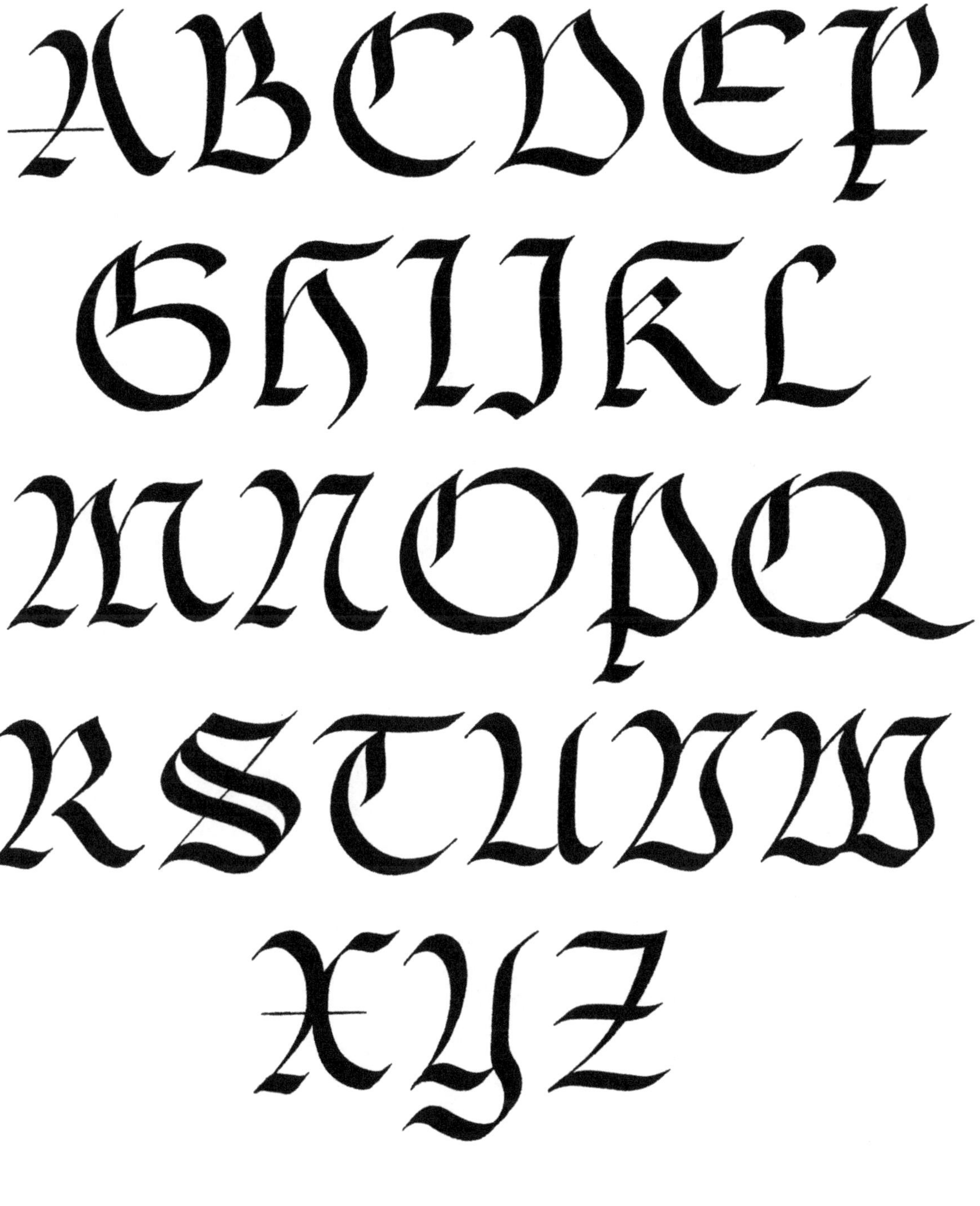

Key Points

pen angle: 45°
x-height: four + two (for ascenders and descenders) pen widths
rhythm: equidistant parallels
O: based on a compressed hexagon

C

E

G

T

O

Q

S

A

blackletter

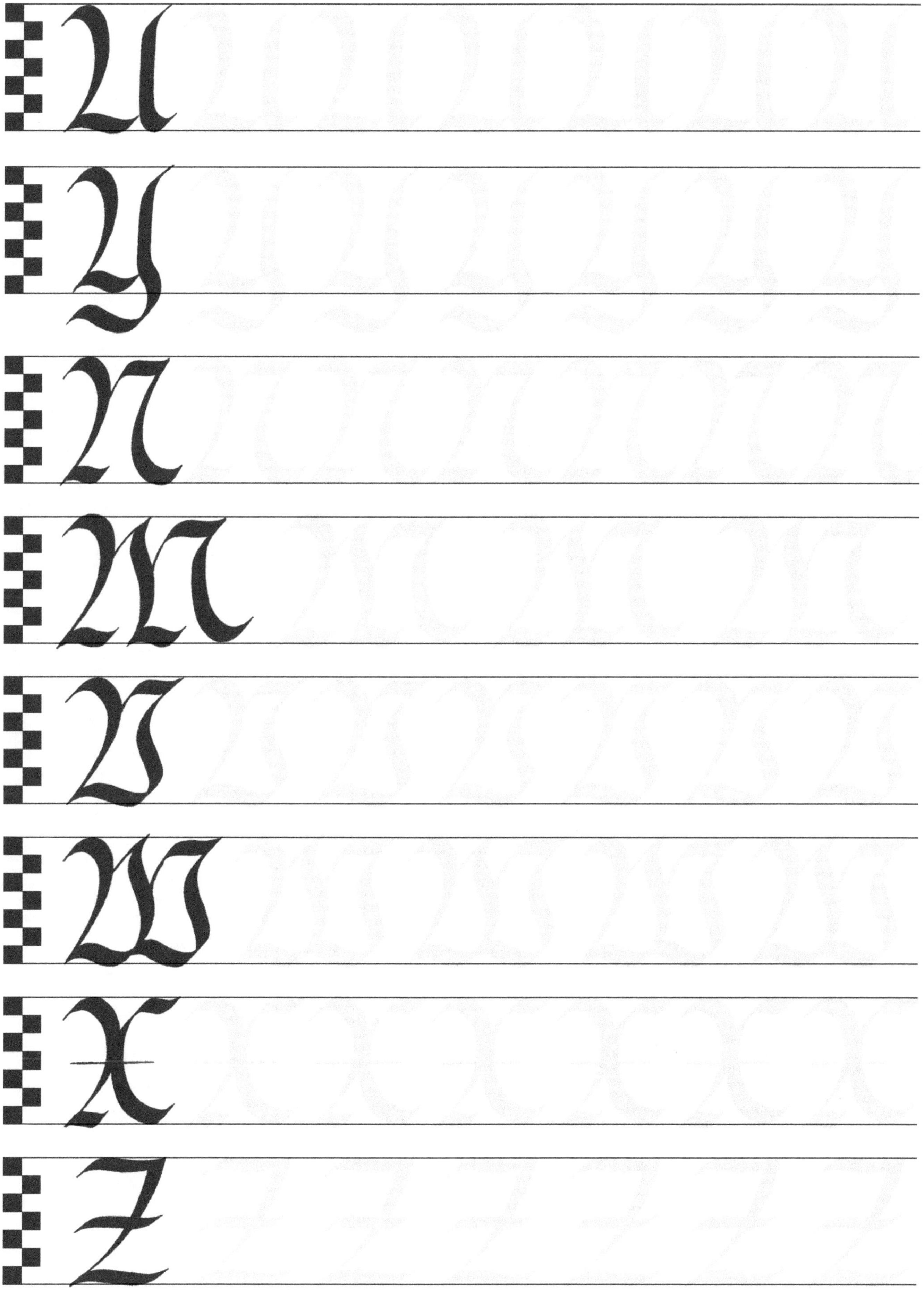

D

P

B

R

K

H

I

J

blackletter

L

P

blackletter

Gothic capitals are wider and rounder than the small letters and unlike every other writing style, they are taller than the ascenders. Gothic majuscules and minuscules were created to work together, and while a row of Roman capitals looks boldly beautiful, a row of Gothic capitals looks lost and unhappy.

These guidelines are designed to practice Gothic with the Pilot Parallel 2.4mm Pen. If you feel like writing with a traditional metal nib, use a Brause 2.5mm, Tape 2.5mm, or Speedball C2.

With a broad-edged pen we thicken our line by holding the pen at an angle. With a pointed pen we simply apply more pressure. Highly responsive to subtle changes in pressure, the pointed pen in the beginner's unsteady hand seems to have its own mind, but in the hand of a master there is much more potential for expression and nuance. Achieve maximum efficiency and minimum opportunity for error by writing with the fewest possible pen lifts.

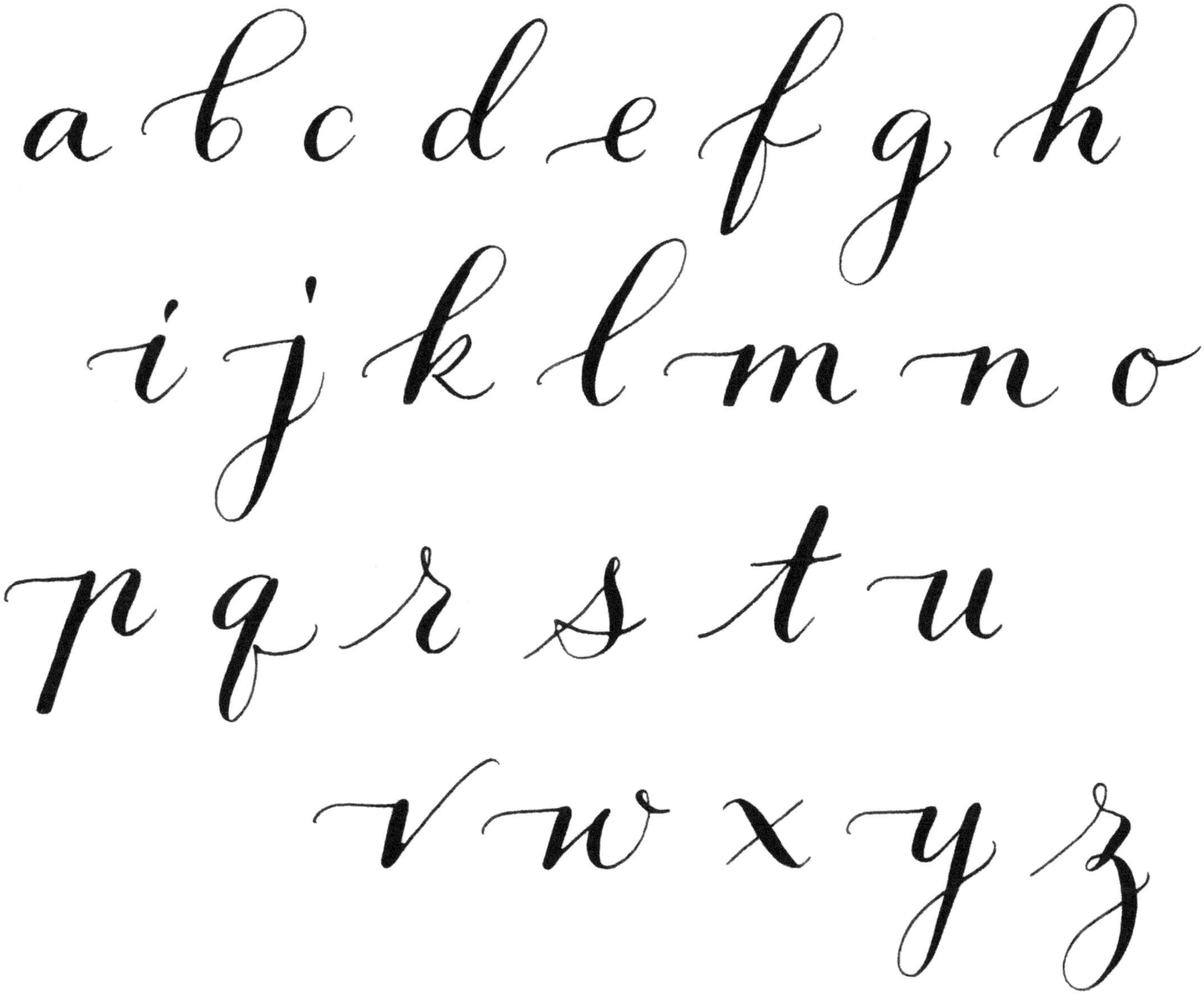

Key Points

pen angle: 55° slope lines on the page, especially for Copperplate
x-height: shorther than ascenders and descenders
rhythm: equidistant parallels
O: based on a compressed, sloping isometric ellipse

Written letters slant to the right, of course, and the right-handed calligrapher can most easily capture this slant by using an oblique nib-holder. A left-handed can achieve the same slant, the correct angle, with a straight nib-holder.

i

t

r

n

m

l

h

k

b

p

g

a

q

d

c

e

o

u

f

s

j

w

v

z

x

y

Majuscules can have a lot of different versions and can be flourished in many ways. But as we always recommend, master simple forms before moving on to the more complex ones.

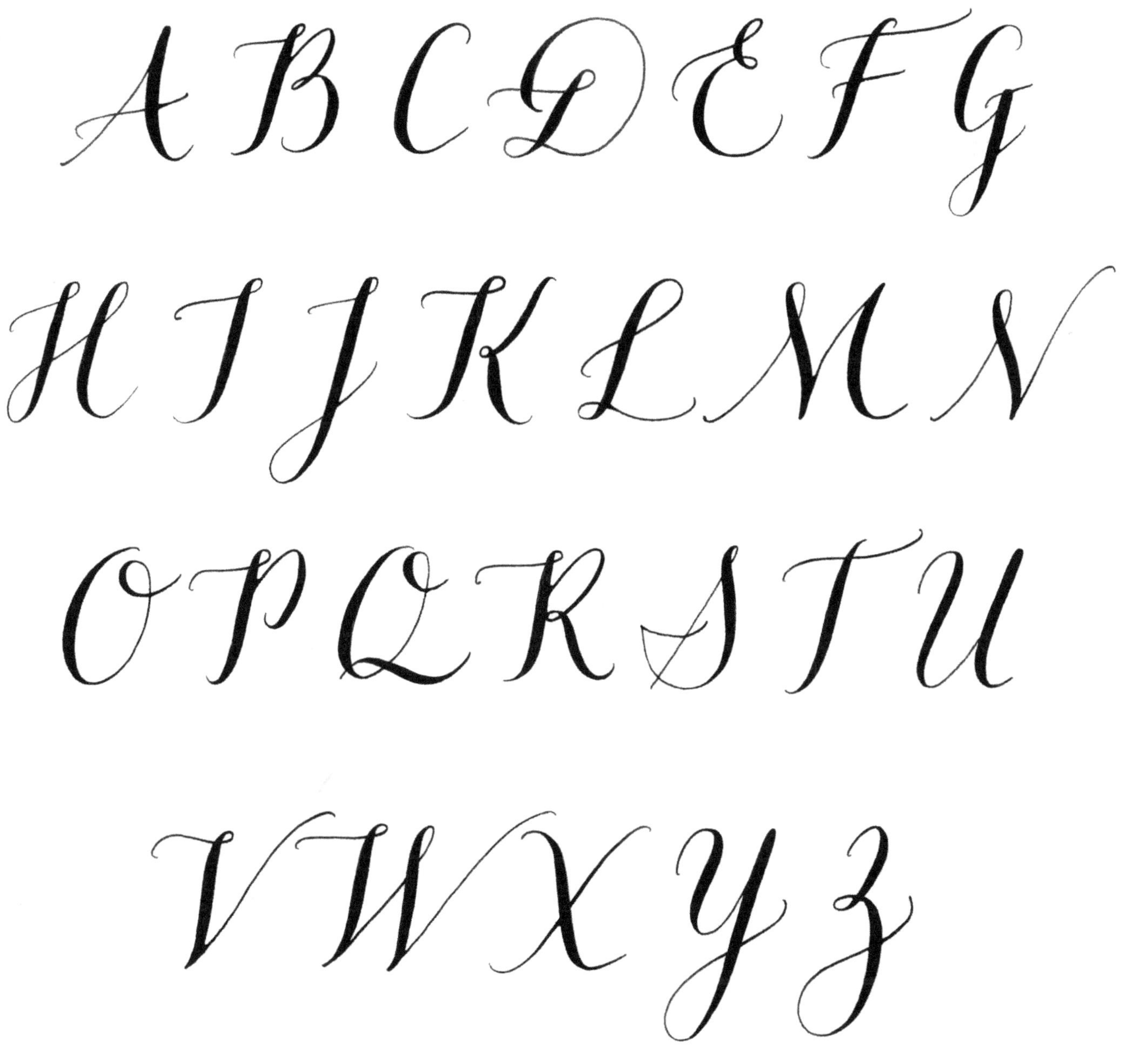

Majuscules are generally more complex and thus harder to execute well. Write your majuscules in one stroke if possible. Thick lines are downstrokes, and that's often a clue as to how to write the majuscules in a single stroke.

B

P

R

D

L

T

F

K

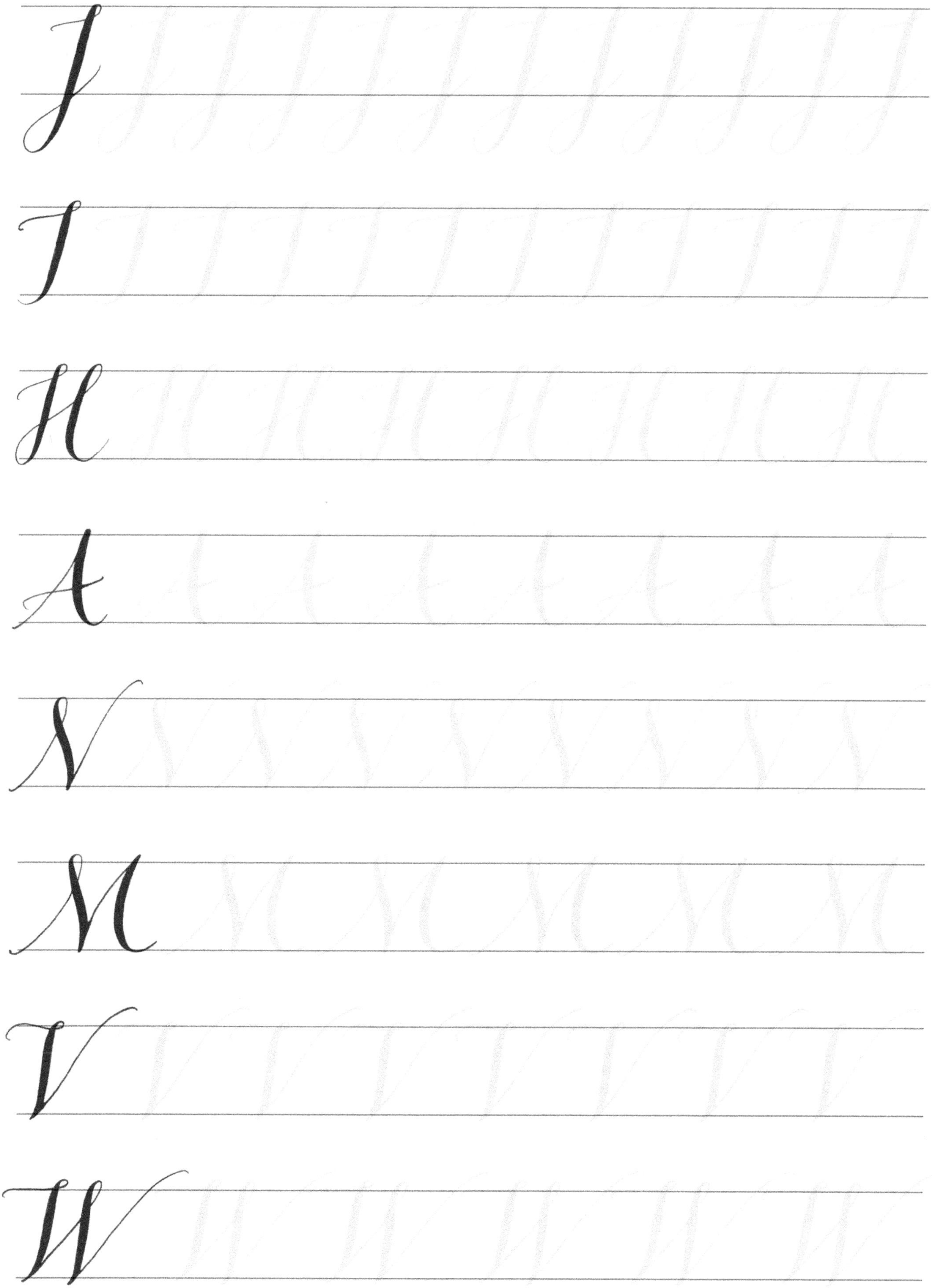
J
T
H
A
N
M
V
W

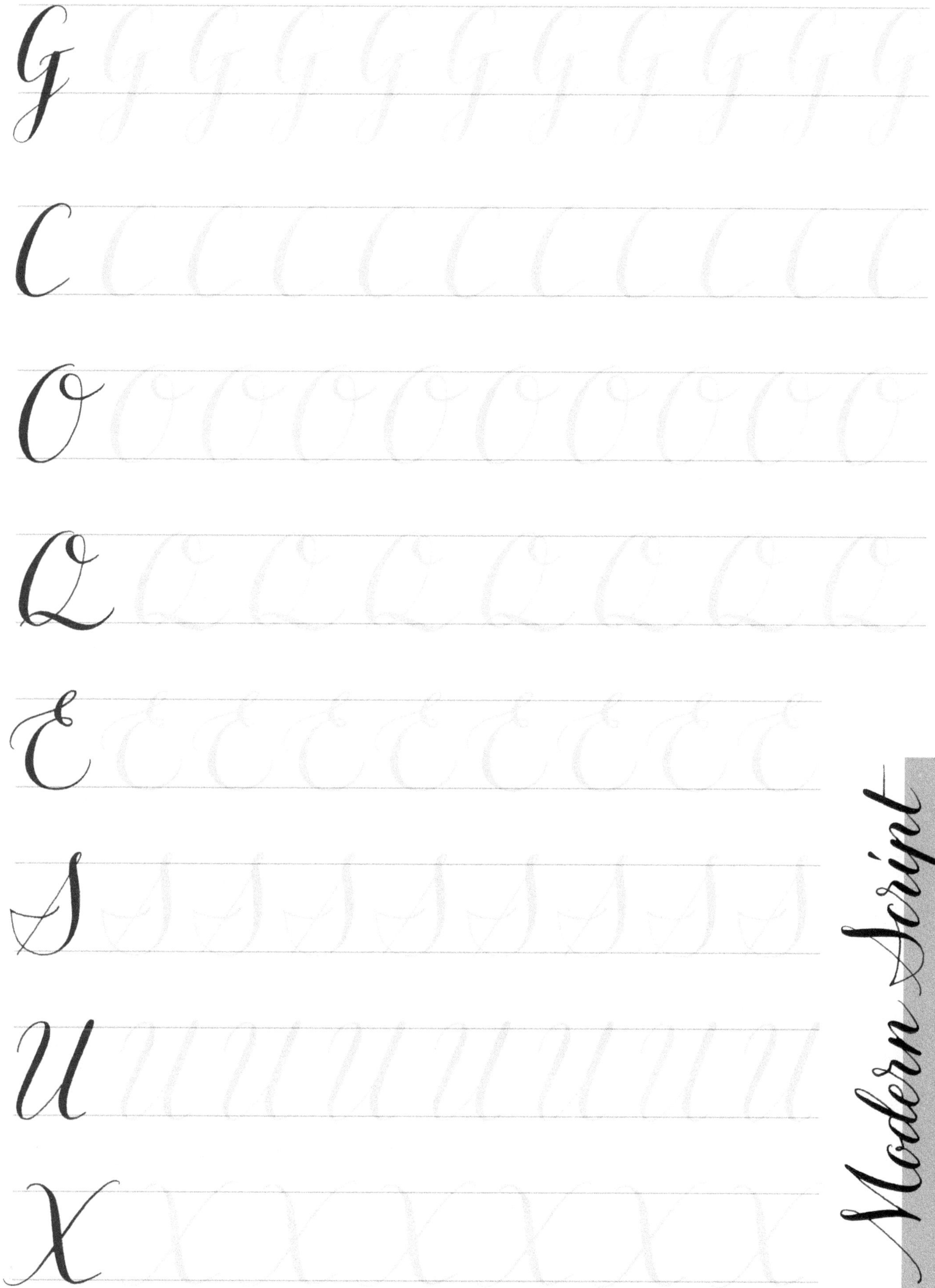

Modern Script

y

z z z z z z z z z z

Lettering

Typography is simply the art of arranging type. You use a particular typeface in typography but not, of course, in calligraphy of lettering.

Calligraphy allows more artistic freedom, as you "write" letters in one smooth stroke as you might sign your name to a check. Lettering allows the most freedom of all; you "draw" letters as you might draw a person's portrait.

"Calligraphy" is obviously a full, rich universe of its own, but it is also an excellent training ground for the aspiring "letterer." A practiced calligrapher knows how to use the right type and size of brush or pen to create the desired effect, can feel when something's not right, knows how to correct it. An aspiring letterer can apply these essential skills to similar, yet very different craft. Knowing the "rules" of pen and ink, the letterer is well-equipped to bend or even break them.

If you can't find an appropriate typeface, if your project cries out for a crazy, unique presentation, "lettering" presents you with unlimited opportunity to create a new every letter, word and sentence.

THE PROCESS

Here's an outline showing the stages of the hand-lettering process from start to finish. Keep in mind that this is not the one and only 'right' way to do it but it is an example that can give you a very good idea of how it's typically done.

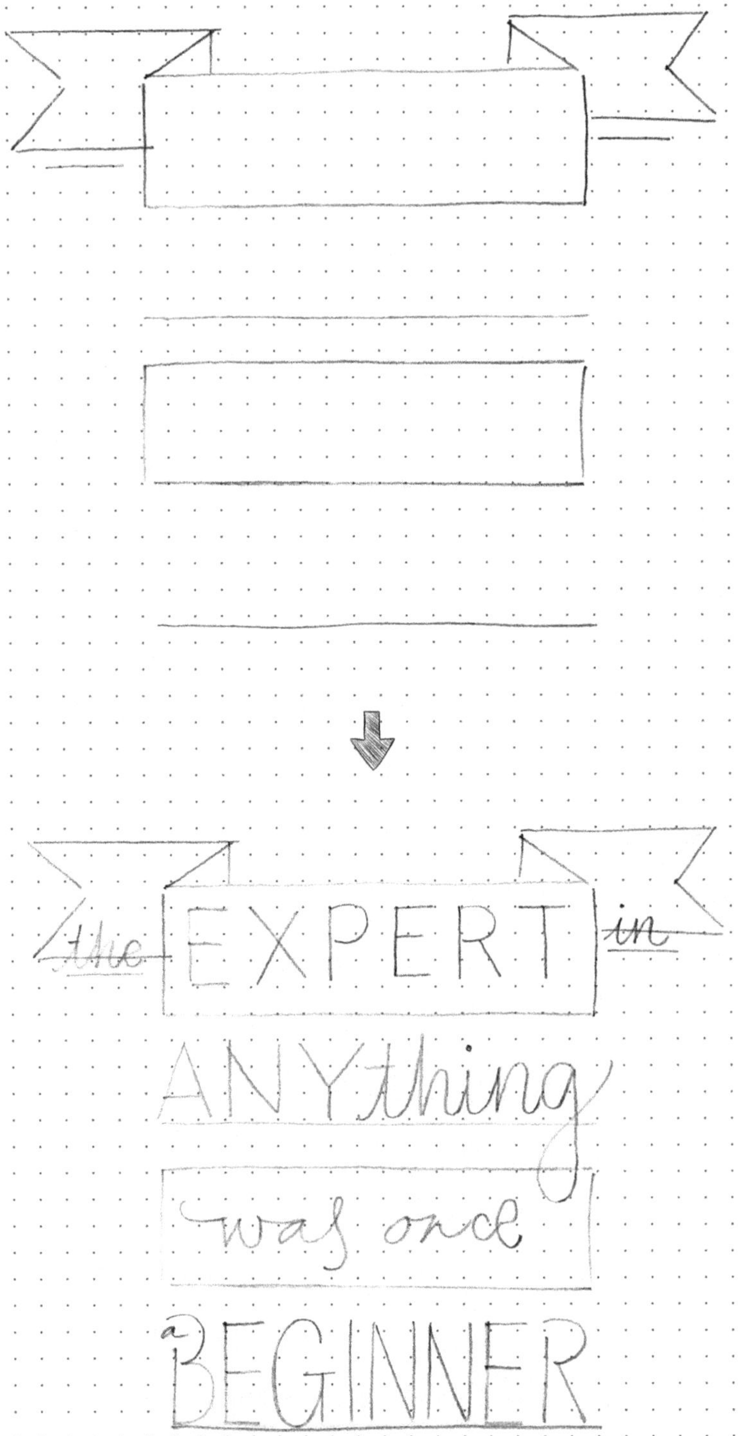

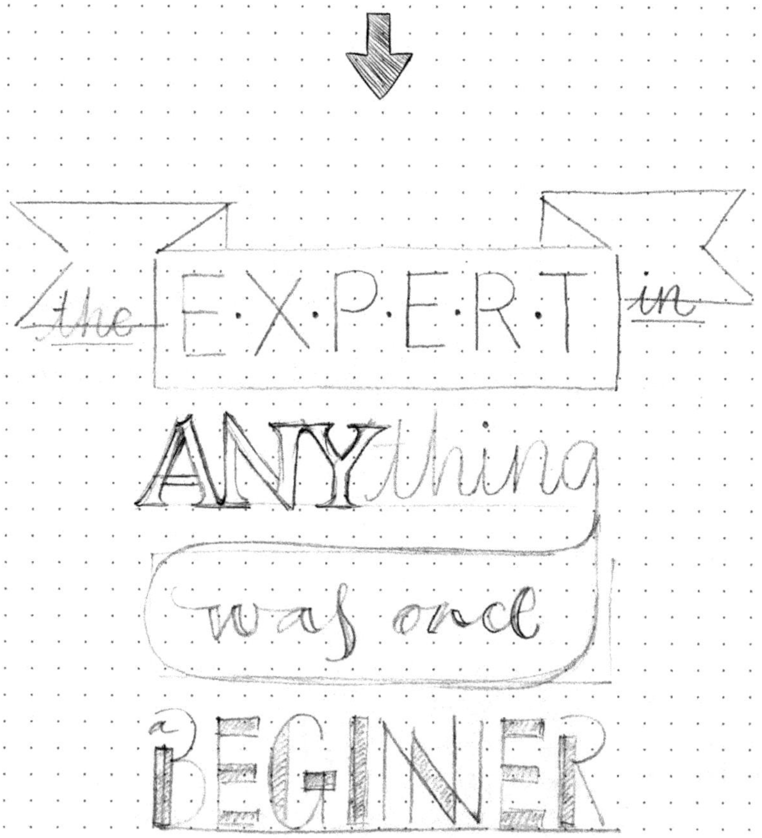
the EXPERT in
ANYthing
was once
a BEGINNER

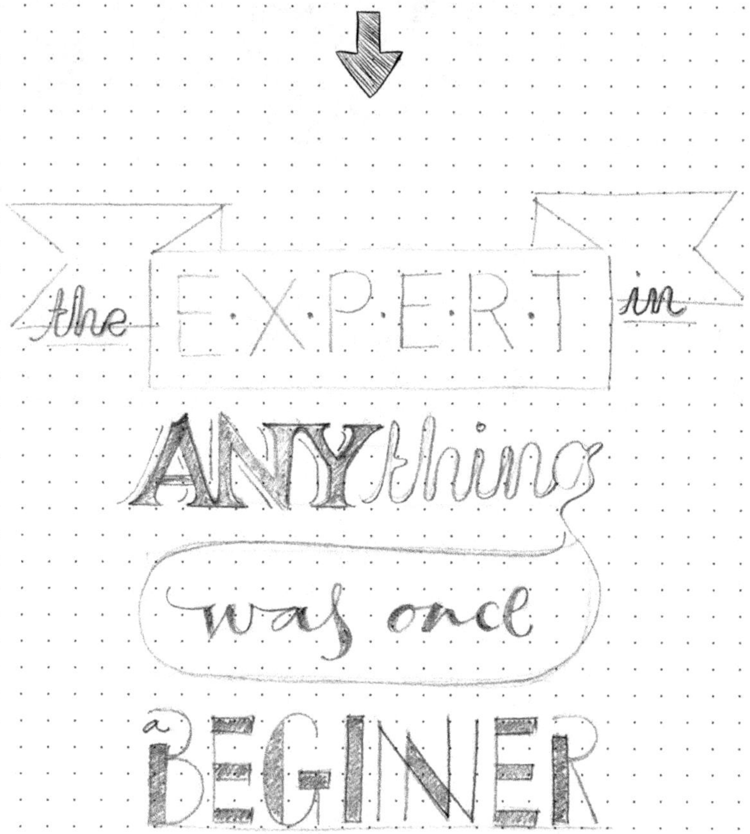
the EXPERT in
ANYthing
was once
a BEGINNER

the EXPERT in ANYthing was once a BEGINNER

HERE WE GO!

1) Choose a phrase. Mentally "size" it so it'll fit your page comfortably.

2) Write your phrase lightly in pencil a few times.
If you're in an especially creative mood, try writing your phrase in an arc, or slanting up or down.

3) "Edit" your favorite sketch.
- can you comfortably combine two letters (or more) into one symbol (a "ligature")?
- do the spaces between letters feel equal?
(Measure the spaces with your calligraphic soul, not with a ruler!)
- can you comfortably add a drop shadow (a shadow-looking thingy), a swash (like you spilled ink), or a serif?
- your phrase should not be heavier here and lighter there.
It should "weigh" the same from beginning to end.

4) Highlight your composition with a border.

5) Now take up your pen and go over your work: directly on top of your drawing, or onto tracing paper.

6) Load your work into Photoshop (optional).
- Scan it at 600 dpi (or higher).
- Open it in Photoshop.
- Clean it up, get rid of any shine or paper texture.
- Adjust levels and hide the cyan channel if you like.
- Open your file in Illustrator, go to Live Trace Options.
Minimize the settings. Play with the threshold. Play with the path fittings. Until you have exactly the effect you're looking for.
- Clicking Enhance gives you a vector image and a palette of colors to enhance your work.

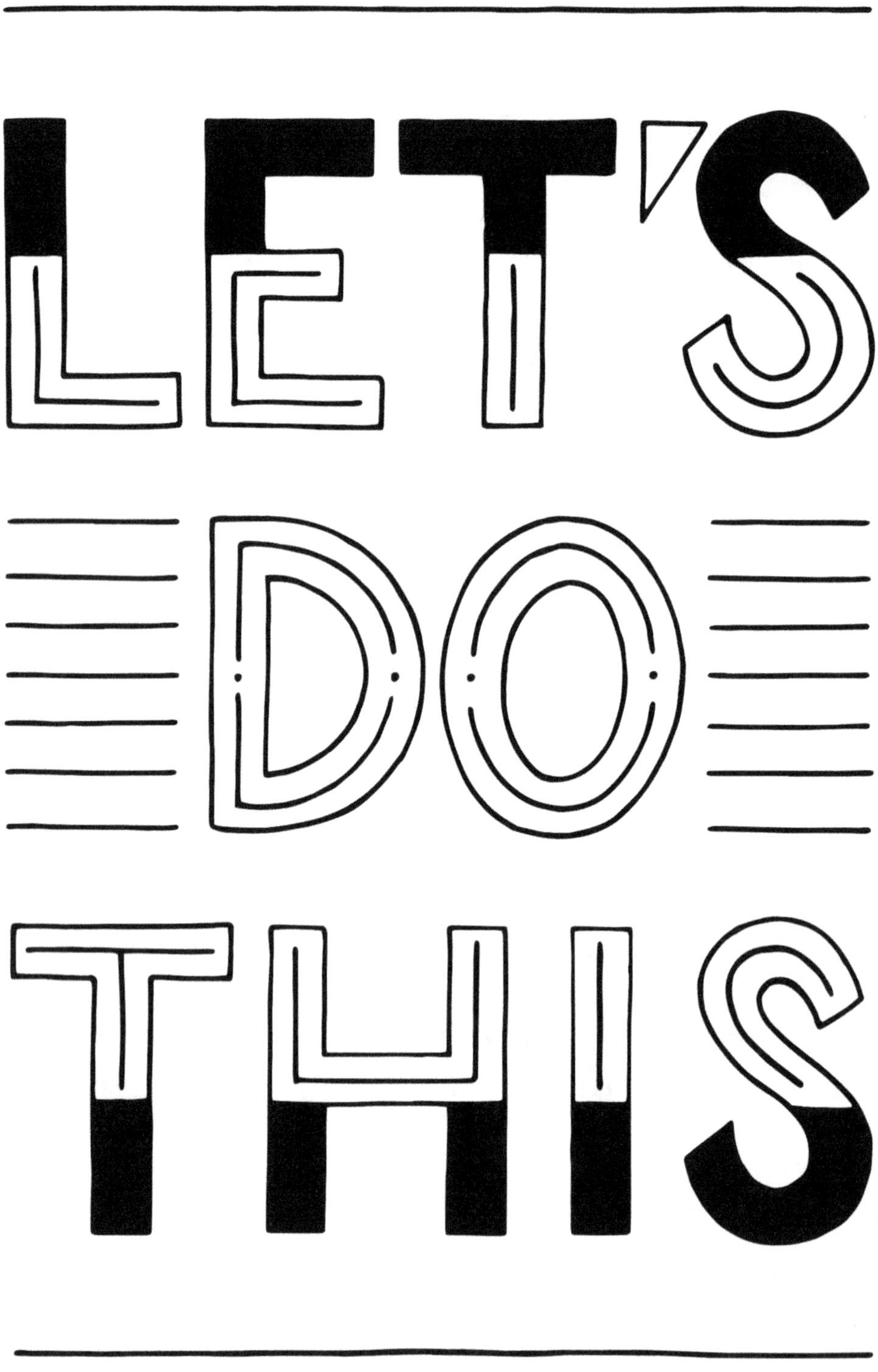

Sans Serif

A sans serif style letter does not have an embellishment added to the end of the stroke. Often used for headings rather than for body text.

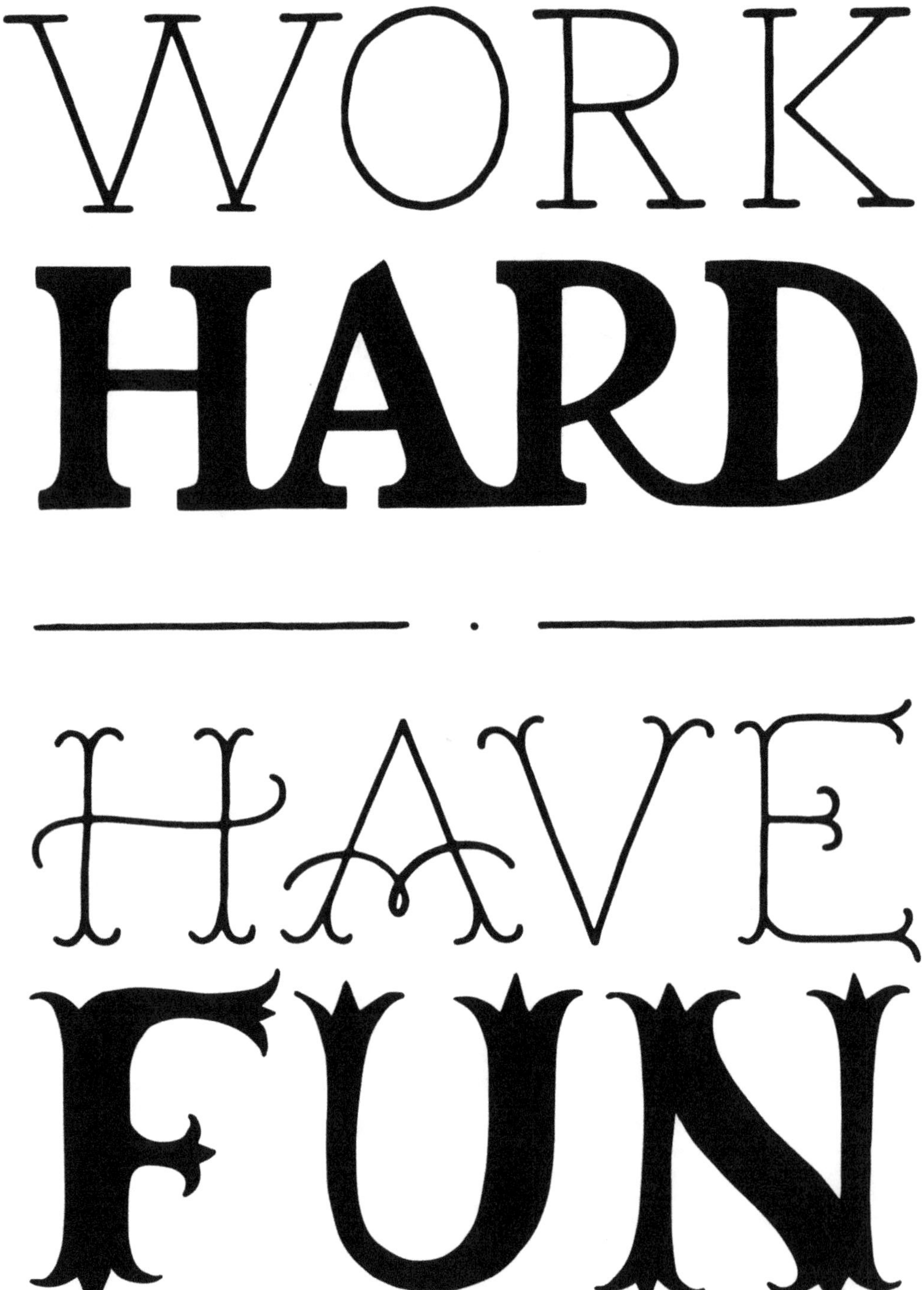

Serif

A serif is a small embellishment added to the end of the strike to make the letter more legible.

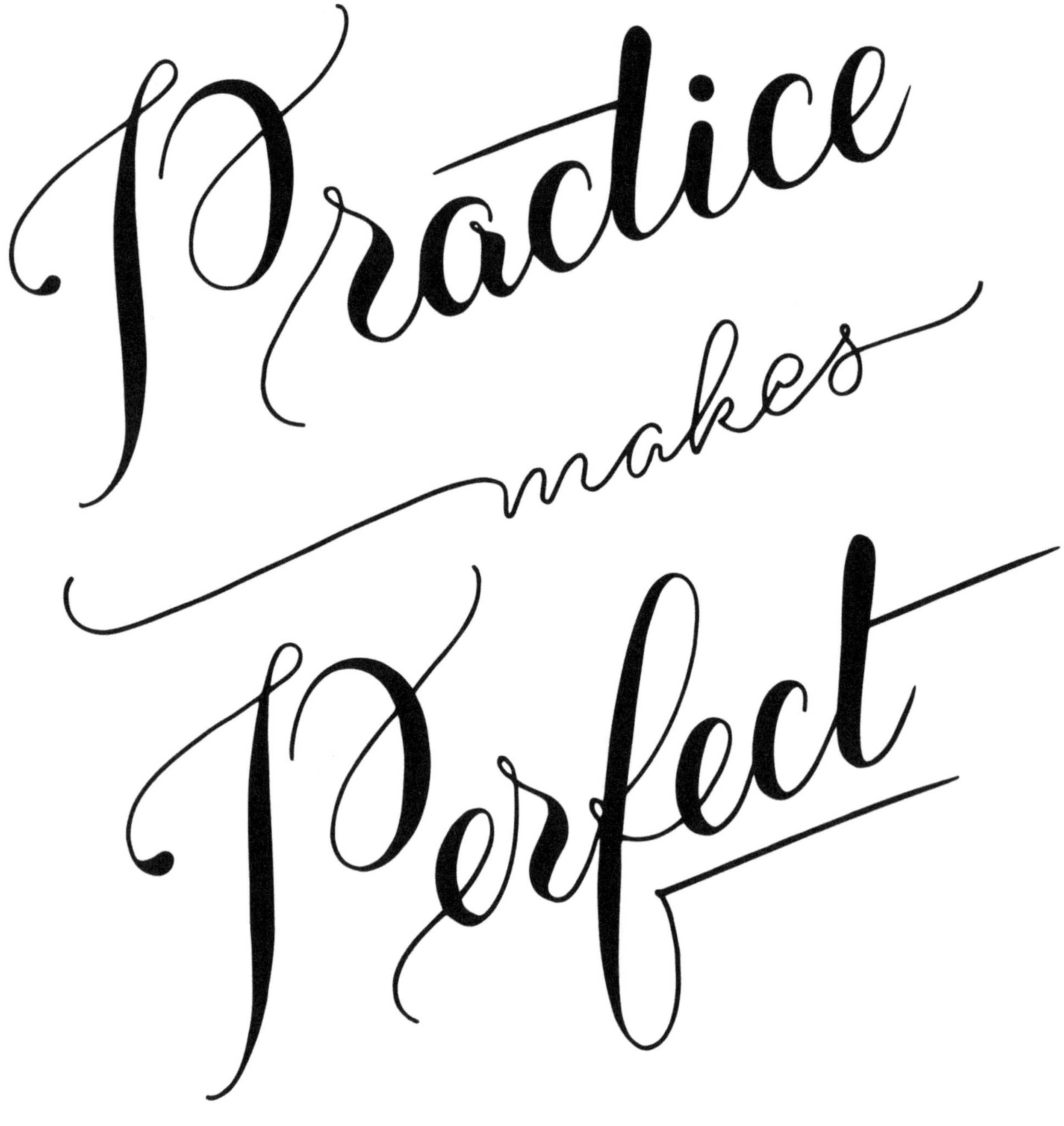

Script

Script lettering is a slanted calligraphic-like style whose strokes sometimes appear to have been created by a wet brush.

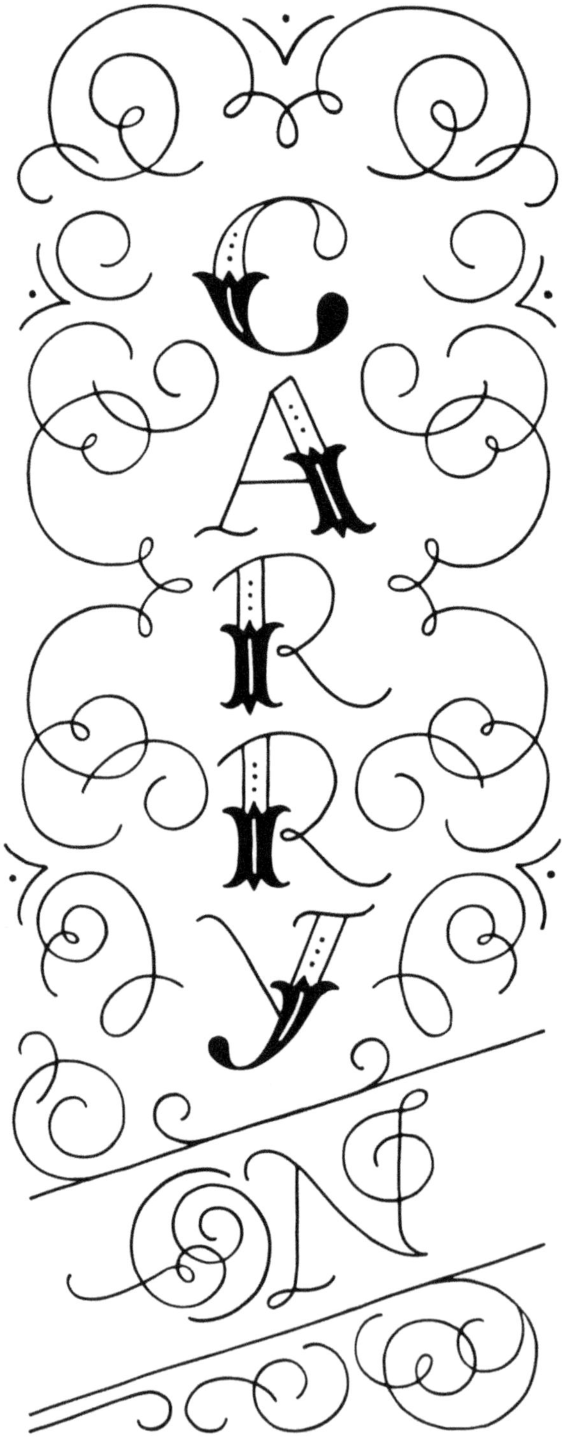

Ornate

Ornate lettering is a highly entertaining and decorative style composed of swirls, serifs, swashes, and other intricate grace notes and often seen in headlines, greeting cards, and on festive occasions.

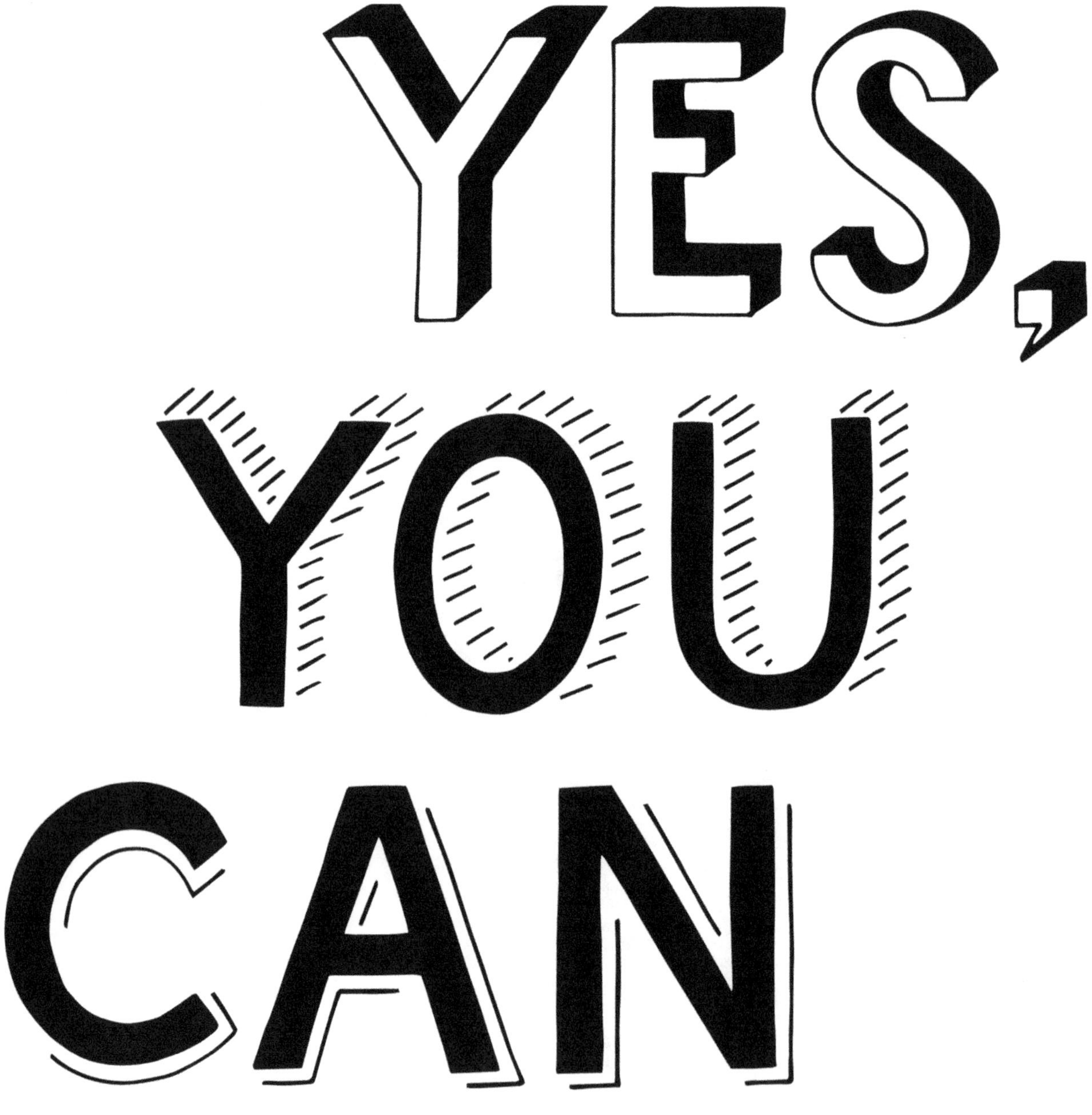

Dimensional

You can add drama to your lettering by using dimensional elements or drop shadows. This style is particularly good for headlines.

GOODBYE AND GOOD LUCK!

Open your eyes and your mind to the creations of our brilliant and inspired brother and sister letterers from the carvers of Trajan's monument to medieval monks and scribes, to those who designed the packaging on your kitchen shelves.

Find your favorites and copy them until you're ready to take off the training wheels and create beautiful letters in your own unique style.

Look for inspiration on YouTube. Join a calligraphy class or an afternoon workshop. (A word from a master can steer you into the most productive channels.) Join a calligraphy society. The Society of Scribes and Illuminators, formed by the students of Edward Johnston in 1921, welcomes professionals and interested amateurs alike.

The rich and wonderful world of letters welcomes you.

One last thing
We would love to hear your feedback about this book!

If you found this book fun and useful, we would be very grateful if you posted a short review on Amazon! Your support does make a difference and we read every review personally.

If you would like to leave a review, just head on over to this book's Amazon page and click "Write a customer review".

Thank you for your support!

CPSIA information can be obtained
at www.ICGtesting.com
Printed in the USA
BVHW011335240320
575846BV00008B/168

9 781951 355234